A GIFT FOR:

_____

FROM:

_____

Published by Hallmark Gift Books,
a division of Hallmark Cards, Inc.,
Kansas City, MO 64141
Visit us on the Web at Hallmark.com.

Editorial Director: Carrie Bolin
Editor: Megan Langford
Art Director: Jan Mastin
Designer: Mary Eakin
Production Designer: Bryan Ring

ISBN: 978-1-59530-661-6
1BOK2137

Printed and bound in China

IS IT *fabulous* IN HERE?

OR IS IT JUST US?

We're together,
and all of a sudden,
it's an *adventure.*

Ours is a friendship
that bursts forth,
spills over,
and possibly requires
dry cleaning.

THE PERFECT PARTY:
good times,
great memories . . .
and no mystery
tattoos!

If they put girlfriends in dressing rooms instead of fluorescent lights, I'd buy a lot more clothes.

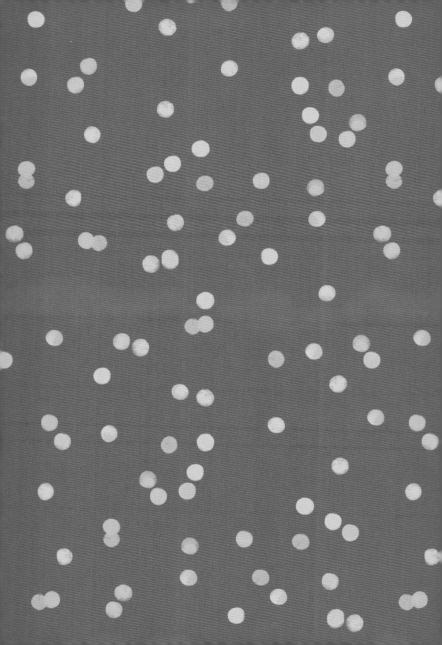

Good friends make
each other laugh . . .
Great friends go for
the snort.

Friends are the
people version of

dessert.

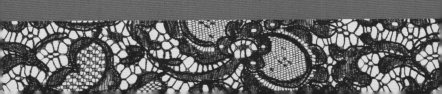

Our history can never
be cleared.

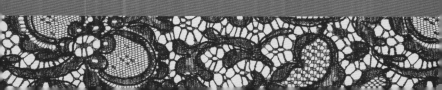

For people like us,
being glam, edgy, fashion-
forward, and smokin' hot
is a full-time job.

It's a miracle
we don't crumble
under pressure.

We're not just good dancers—we're Jumbotron good dancers.

Everything in moderation.
Except fun. And sugar.
An excess of those is always OK.

I like to think that
we are each other's
moral compass,
which is bad news
for both of us.

It's a fine line between *friend* and accomplice.

Look at us. We're cool, we're smart, we're funny—
we're just two peas in a really awesome pod.

Never, ever waste a good song.

Friends are the salt of the earth
around an extra-large

margarita.

Some people were born to stand out.

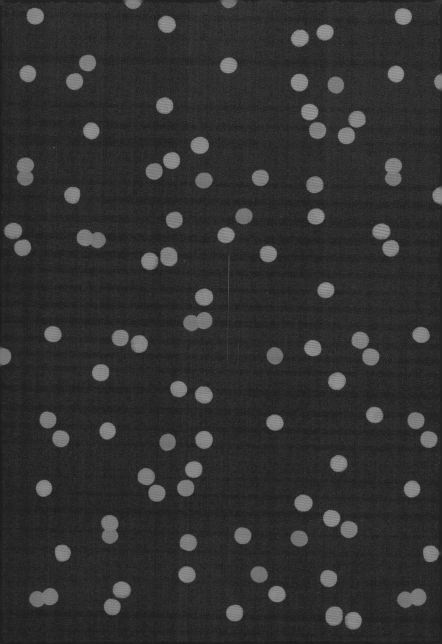

Make new friends but
keep the old.
They're the ones with the
embarrassing pictures.

Stone-cold fox
is a state of mind!

Friends have funny
the way a hot fudge
sundae has sweet.

A good friend
will keep all your secrets.
Or not be able to remember
them. Either way, I'm your gal.

Whoever says you can't have
it all has never been to the
frozen yogurt store with me.

I think our souls
have had enough
chicken soup. Let's
open some wine.

Whole self in? Check.
Moving and shaking all
about? *Very* check.

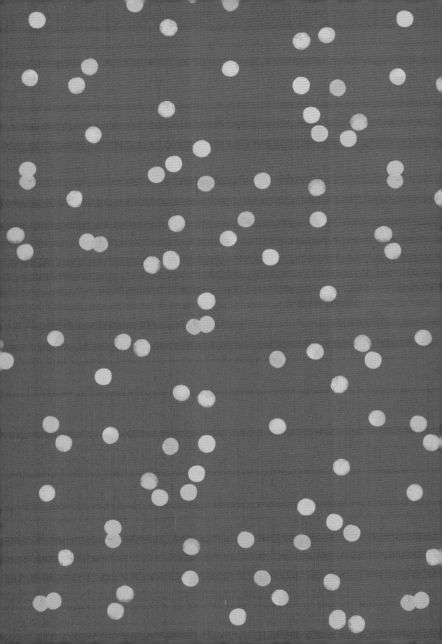

Two wrongs don't
make a right,
but they make a
much better story.

Live it up today!
(Live it down tomorrow.)

Any hour spent with friends is

"happy hour."

It's good to be
the life of the party.
It's even better to
be the life of . . .
well, LIFE!

Follow your heart
more than the rules.

Choose happiness.
Or choose queso dip.
Same thing, really.

Friends maintain
a strict open-door
(and open-wine) policy.

Not every day can be a party,
but every day *can* have
music, laughter, and friends,
and that's just as good.

Let the *shenanigans* begin!

Kick up heels.
Let hair down.
Bring friends along!

Real friends
don't call carrot
sticks a snack.

When in doubt, go all out!

Somewhere between
"had a nice time"

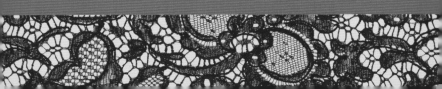

and "cha-cha-cha'd on the table"—that's the party *sweet* spot!

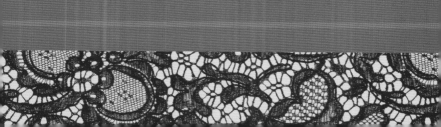

I'm not especially good at wrestling plastic wrap or folding fitted sheets, but when it comes to celebrating people I love, I've got the touch!

When she was good,
she was very, very good,
but when she was bad . . .

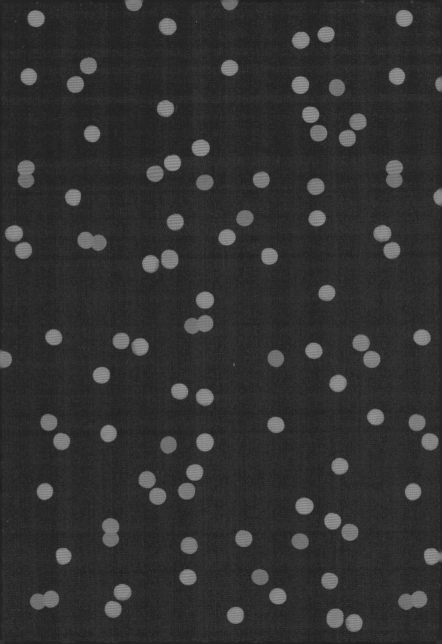

Every girl needs her own personal anthem— something she can sing along and wave a lighter to every time she hears it.

Not sure how I got

lucky enough

to have the friends I do,
but I'm just going with it.

Where do we get jobs
as ice-cream inspectors?
We'd kick ass at that.

Ever start having
fun and just sort of
forget how to stop?
Don't worry.
Happens to the
best of us.

Better a life well lived than a house well scrubbed.

We never met a problem
a Girls' Night Out
couldn't solve.

I'm a glass-half-full kind of person (though a glass all full would be better).

Life is a party.
Bring confetti!

If you have enjoyed this book
or it has touched your life in some way,
we would love to hear from you.

Please send your comments to:
Hallmark Book Feedback
P.O. Box 419034
Mail Drop 100
Kansas City, MO 64141

Or e-mail us at:
booknotes@hallmark.com